197

CONTENTS

Painting on cover: Claude Monet, *Impression, Sunrise* (1872), detail.

Graphic design: Sandra Brys

First published in the United States in 1995 by Chelsea House Publishers.

© 1993 by Casterman, Tournai

First Printing

1 3 5 7 9 8 6 4 2

ISBN 0-7910-2823-2

ART FOR CHILDREN

THE IMPRESSIONISTS

By Yolande Blanquet

Illustrations by Christian Maucter

Translated by John Goodman

CHELSEA HOUSE PUBLISHERS

NEW YORK • PHILADELPHIA

The day I was born, the fairies lighted on my cradle and declared, "He will live only for the arts. He will be a painter or an art historian."

Astonished, my parents looked at the strange being to whom they had given life. Neither of them knew very much about art; they could scarcely tell the difference between a Leonardo da Vinci and a Pablo Picasso. So from where they stood, they might as well have given birth to a Martian! But being determined to understand their offspring, they began to visit museums and libraries. Books piled up on shelves and tables from the bedroom to the living room, and even in the kitchen and the bathroom. I found myself between books about the painters Raphael and Piero della Francesca, the Brueghels and Jan Vermeer, Henri Matisse and Piet Mondrian. As I grew up, I became acquainted with everything from early cave paintings to the latest graffiti.

Now everyone's saying that it's art history for me.

I have red hair, but I didn't get it from either of my parents. It was a gift from the fairies, a kind of tribute to the flamboyant suns of Vincent Van Gogh.

Obviously I'm going to talk to you about painting. My buddies always say to me, "Painting is boring, it's for old people." That's crazy! It's terrific. Getting to know an artist or an artistic movement, learning how to approach a body of work and dig into it a bit, is a most exciting adventure.

You'll see! In the pages of this book I'll introduce you to a temple. Temples are great places for adventures, don't you think? I have in my possession all the keys to this one, and here are some hints that might help you guess what I'm talking about: the banks of the Seine River; a tube of color; a rower.

Answer: My temple is Impressionism.

First of all, we have to find a name for you. As for me, I'm Tom. As for you, I'll call you the Eye—no, Oculus. That's the Latin word for eye, and it sounds more impressive.

Don't be impatient: any adventure calls for at least a little preparation. A bit of geography, a bit of history. What map will we need? One of France. One that includes Paris, Argenteuil, Chatou, Bougival, Fontainebleau, Barbizon, and the Normandy coast. What period is in question? The middle of the 19th century, 1863 to be precise, when a slight tremor made the lights in the Palace of Industry flicker on and off.

That's where the official Salon exhibition was held.

So let's be off!

Oculus, do you know what kind of painters were fashionable in that period?

I'll help you out a bit: painters of goddesses, grapes, Greek columns, and little angels.

And then there were two great masters, one classic, the other romantic. Let me introduce you to Jean-Dominique Ingres and Eugène Delacroix. Controversy raged at the official Salon exhibition. The supporters of Ingres and those of Delacroix were virtually at each others throats. Everyone had to choose: Ingres or Delacroix? Depending on who was asking the question and how you responded, you were either patted on the back or knocked in the head.

Ingres was the embodiment of classicism and a very great draftsman. For him, painting was above all a question of drawing; color was a secondary consideration.

Jean-Dominique Ingres, *The Grand Odalisque*, 1814. Oil on canvas, 2 feet 11 inches × 5 feet 4 inches.

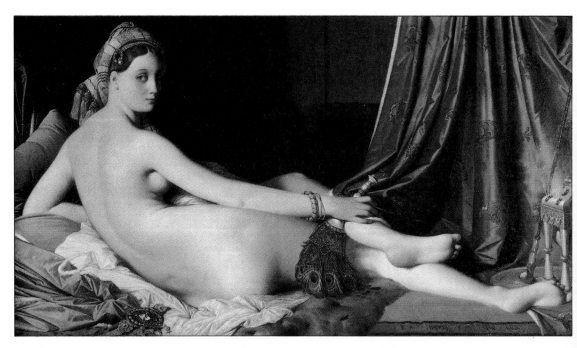

The female nude was frequently represented in Western art. Here the model looks at us but seems frozen for all time.

Delacroix, by contrast, was a romantic painter, favoring passion and brashness. For him, color was master. In his work everything is in motion; things are constantly changing and evolving. But don't be afraid, the lion in the painting won't jump out at you!

Eugène Delacroix, *Lion Hunt*, 1855. Oil on canvas, 2 feet 3 inches × 3 feet 4 inches.

In 1863 the Salon jury was so demanding that the Emperor Napoléon III sponsored the first Salon des Refusés, or exhibition of rejected artists. On its walls one could see works by Édouard Manet, Camille Pissarro, Barthold Jongkind, Henri Fantin-Latour, Paul Cézanne, and many others who would later become the Impressionists, the pioneers of modern art.

But in 1863 they didn't give pleasure or move their viewers, they provoked laughter. Yes, Oculus, hundreds of people happily made fun of Claude Monet, Pierre-Auguste Renoir, and Cézanne.

One work in particular provoked a huge scandal. This was the *Déjeuner sur l'herbe,* or *Luncheon on the Grass,* by Edouard Manet. This artist had painted a nude woman in the company of two fully dressed men, which led to accusations of indecency. But a more important aspect of the painting was that it showed middle-class individuals in conversation during a picnic.

Let's be cleverer than these visitors, Oculus, and get right to essentials. The fairies didn't light on my cradle for nothing, thank you! The *Luncheon on the Grass* was the first light-toned painting. It inaugurated a new way of looking at nature. Manet used light colors and quick, broad brushstrokes, and he paid little attention to the positioning of the body. His figures are of the 19th century,

just like himself. He was fed up with the ancient world and wanted to paint his own period.

Two important steps in the direction of Impressionism had now been taken: a lightening of the palette, and the representation of the present. But a third and crucial development had yet to occur, and it was an important one: painting in the open air!

This idea had imposed itself in stages. Initially, sketches were made on site and then worked up in the studio. Gustave Courbet worked like this, although his tonal range was still quite dark. But his ambition to make a vivid, realist art greatly influenced the Impressionists.

Édouard Manet, *Luncheon on the Grass* (*Le Dejeuner sur l'herbe*), 1863. Oil on canvas, 6 feet 10 inches × 8 feet 8 inches.

Henri-Julien-Félix Rousseau, Jean-Baptiste-Camille Corot, Charles-François Daubigny, Narcisse-Virgile Diaz de La Peña, and Jean-François Millet were also precursors. You couldn't take even a step in their beloved Barbizon Forest without tripping over an easel, for the nearby inns were full of these "sons of light," as they were called by a journalist of the day. They didn't finish their canvases in the open air but wanted "to look at nature with humility and paint it as it appears under changing skies and weather conditions, trying to capture the transparence of the atmosphere."

We are now at the threshold of the temple. But we can't enter it without paying tribute to some of its guardian spirits.

First there was Eugène Boudin. He didn't have an impressive name like you do, but nonetheless he said things of great importance: "Everything painted on site has a strength, a power, a vivacity of touch that cannot be duplicated in the studio." He painted seascapes and landscapes, and he was convinced that open-air painting was the only method for getting such pictures to come out right. It was he who encouraged Monet, at age sixteen, to make his first paintings. Until that point young Claude had been known

in the town of Le Havre as a caricaturist.

He later said, "It was thanks to Eugène Boudin that I became a painter."

We should be grateful to you, Eugène: Monet was a pretty good caricaturist, but he was to become an essential member of the Impressionist group.

Monet's second teacher was Barthold Jongkind, another painter of seascapes and also enamored of nature. He made sketches like the Barbizon painters, but he also executed watercolors attentive to the play of natural light and changes in the weather. His work was more nervous and uneasy than Boudin's and had a precise yet agitated quality that fascinated Monet. The latter would later say: "It is to him that I owe the definitive education of my eye." In a similar way, I'm going to educate you, Oculus, by initiating you into the mysteries of art.

Two more guardian spirits, and then we'll be ready to enter the realm of light.

What do you say we cross the English Channel, our nose in the clouds, floating on our backs?

Sometimes I write poetry, like my friend Charles Baudelaire, who said: "I love clouds, clouds passing by . . . how marvelous clouds are!"

"Who do you love best, mysterious man? Tell me. Your father, your mother, your sister, or your brother?"

"I have neither father nor mother, sister nor brother."

"And friends?"

"You have just used a word whose meaning is still unknown to me."

"Your country?"

"I do not know its latitude."

"Beauty?"

"I would love her willingly, goddess and immortal."

"Gold?"

"I hate it like you hate God."

"Ah! Then what is it you love, extraordinary stranger?"

"I love clouds, clouds passing by, over there . . . and over there. How wonderful clouds are!"

On the other side of the channel, a certain John Constable had the same obsession: he spent entire days painting clouds, analyzing the slightest variations in their shapes and colors. The countryside was his other favorite subject. He set out to capture in his paintings "the light, the dew, the breeze, the freshness and bloom of nature. None of which has been painted before. No two days are alike, no two hours, even, and no two leaves on a tree have been identical since the creation of the world." During a trip to London, Pissarro and Monet were able to see his paintings.

John Constable, *Clouds*, 1822. Oil on paper, 1 foot 3 inches × 1 foot 7 inches.

They also saw paintings by William Turner. Ah! Just look at *Rain, Steam and Speed*! It might seem to be every bit as impressionist as all the Impressionist paintings we're about to discover. But prudence is in order. This painter was to Impressionism as a book traveler is to a real globe trotter. His skull was his open-air realm: he had all the light in the world in his brain.

Monet and Pissarro were seduced by his paintings at first. But they subsequently denied his having influenced them, referring to the "exhuberant romanticism of his imagination." As for myself, I'm sure that, unbeknownst to themselves, thieves against their will, they appropriated something of the hazy colors, the impression of movement, the reflections, and even the evocative dream-like atmosphere typical of works by this English master.

J.M.W. Turner, *Rain,
Steam and Speed*, 1844.
Oil on canvas, 3 feet × 4
feet.

The temple is within sight, Oculus, but first I have to tell you about the birth of the Impressionist group. And let's have a bite to eat, too—a starving eye doesn't see clearly. This spot looks just right.

The setting? It's dawn; an orange sun burns through the morning mist. On the horizon, cranes; closer by, a boat carrying two figures. Where are we? In the studio of Félix Nadar on April 15, 1874, in front of *Impression, Sunrise* by Monet, at the opening of the first exhibition of the Independent Artists. That's the name under which Renoir, Monet, Pissarro, Cézanne, Alfred Sisley, Berthe Morisot, and Edgar Degas banded together. It was an apt name, for they wanted above all to preserve their independence. This artists' cooperative held regular meetings and had a set of rules, a treasurer, and a president: Renoir.

The name Impressionism derives from a dismissive joke. On seeing *Impression, Sunrise*, a well-accepted painter brought to the show by a journalist friend cried out: "Impression, I was sure of it; since it impresses me, I said to myself, 'impression' must be in the title." The journalist saw his chance, and titled his review article "Exhibition of the Impressionists."

A funny sort of christening! But the name stuck, and most members of the group adopted it—except for Degas, who always rejected it.

The first exhibition of the Independent Artists was mounted in response to the official Salon by young artists who were tired of being rejected and misunderstood. They wanted to let the public make up its own mind. But they got a nasty surprise, for this public wasn't receptive, either. It responded with remarks such as "I understand very well, thank you. To paint like this all you have to do is load up a pistol with paints, fire at the canvas, and sign it. Now there's a work of art for you!"

The Independents mounted eight ex-

hibitions. The participants varied somewhat from year to year, for there were tensions within the group. Monet and Renoir showed only four times, but Pissarro took part in all eight exhibitions. In fact, it was thanks to his determination that so many shows were organized.

Claude Monet, *Impression, Sunrise,* 1872. Oil on canvas, 1 foot 7 inches × 2 feet 1 inch.

Auguste Renoir, *The Boating Party*, 1881. Oil on canvas, 4 feet 3 inches × 5 feet 8 inches.

Here we are in front of the temple, but where's the entrance? Let's take a stroll around the building. Shush! Listen, do you hear the music? You have our bag, Oculus, dig out the first key. Chatou will be our jungle. Yes, it's working!

AAAAAAAAaaaaaa! Tom as Tarzan, what do you think! Instead of tom-tom drums we hear a dance band, and the only snakes to be met with here are garlands of lights. Only adventures of the heart are to be had in this place. On Sunday afternoons, Parisians go to the suburban tavern known as La Grenouillère ("the frog pond") or to the restaurant called La Fournaise. Boatmen drink white wine under the canopy while chatting with bright-eyed young women.

Renoir receives us with his usual warmth: "For me a painting should be something lovable, joyous, and pretty, yes, pretty! There are enough disturbing things in this life, we don't need to make any more," he proclaims. Let's enter into his easy-going, refreshing world. The young woman holding the little dog is Aline, his future wife. The young man sitting backwards on the chair is Gustave Caillebotte.

Many artists of the period painted their friends, and sometimes they included themselves in their canvases.

What if Renoir were to paint my portrait? Though familiar with red hair, he'd have a hard time capturing all the shades of red, orange, and yellow that shimmer in my mop.

21. Rueil. — Ile de Chatou, vue pri

The Fornaise restaurant in Chatou was the setting for *The Boating Party*. It was a favorite gathering place for the cultured and wealthy. It still stands today.

No, we can't take a break, Oculus, we've got to forge head to another jungle. This one is Argenteuil. In fact, we're already there. We're in the thick of it, floating right up against the boats.

First, a few words about Argenteuil. It's a bit like Chatou, a delicious place where one can spend a pleasant afternoon boating and an evening on the dance floor.

In 1874 Manet, Monet, and Renoir came here to work; they sometimes pitched their easels in the same spot. It was here that Manet really discovered the joys of working in the open.

Often, the similarity of the names Manet and Monet led to their being confused with one another—and their paintings, too. But I hope we won't make this dreadful mistake; the fairies would be very irritated with me!

The work of these two artists is quite

At an international exposition, two seascapes by Monet were hung beside a canvas by Manet, who received several letters complimenting him on his seascapes! At the time, he had not yet met the future creator of the *Waterlillies* paintings. He was furious. The incident led to an article featuring the following quip: "Monet or Manet? Monet. But we owe this Monet to Manet. Bravo, Monet! Thank you, Manet!"

Édouard Manet, *Argenteuil*, detail.

different. Manet was seduced by the Impressionists and sometimes painted their subject matter, but he always emphasized drawing and clarity of form. In the painting above, the figures are so precisely captured that they could be portraits.

You're right, Oculus, their painting styles are quite different, too. Manet's conveys movement. If his paintings sometimes lack detail, this very quality creates in them a sense of activity and life.

Édouard Manet, *Argenteuil*, 1874. Oil on canvas, 4 feet 11 inches × 4 feet 4 inches.

Monet's paintings are broken up into contrasting tones. If you stick your nose up against his canvases they don't make any sense, but when you move away from them everything comes together, as if by magic. His is a unifying touch. It isn't finicky about details. It is faithful to the artist's vision. Monet takes in an impression and his choppy, rhythmic brushstrokes pin it down on the canvas.

In Argenteuil in 1874, Monet acquired a boat in which he could travel, live, and paint. This made it possible for him to make a close study of the play of light over water. Water, water, water, my friend, is a marvellous magic mirror in which life becomes livelier and is made to dance. Monet was always fascinated by it. He even said that he'd like to be "buried in a buoy."

Claude Monet, *The Bridge at Argenteuil,* detail.

In *The Bridge at Argenteuil,* the river occupies two-thirds of the canvas. Contours disappear in it, shapes become fluid. Color is the most concrete element, making it possible to read the painting. This work features the fragmented touch typical of the artist, and it was developed to capture the effects of light over water. But it would prove suitable for depictions of other things as well.

Claude Monet, *The Bridge at Argenteuil,* 1874. Oil on canvas, 2 feet × 2 feet 7 inches.

Camille Pissarro,
**Boulevard Montmartre,
Night Effect**, 1897. Oil
on canvas, 1 foot 9
inches × 2 feet 2 inches.

Temples have their traps, Oculus, their mirrors and screens of water that can deceive us. We must be careful when it comes to reflections, even though this theme was dear to the Impressionists.

Let's not go too fast, Oculus, there's danger here, just as there is for moths, those little insects that flutter around lamps. Like them, we might burn our wings if we move too close to those lights in the night that punctuate the boulevard like so many ripples in the water. Pissarro covers his canvases with little strokes that make his forms quiver. The paving is treated as if it were the Seine, and the carriages are reflected in it. The ground is wet, and the view is blurred as if seen through a curtain of rain.

Shall we analyse his style, Oculus?

It is divided and vibrant. It lets the forms breathe. Towards the end of his life his brushstrokes would become smaller and airier, a bit like a field of dots.

In the 1870s, young artists gathered around Manet at the Cafe Guerbois on the Boulevard des Batignolles. This "Batignolles Group" included Degas, Fantin-Latour, Renoir, Monet, Pissarro, Émile Zola, and Charles Baudelaire. They later came to prefer the Nouvelle Athenes, where they came to be known as the "Intransigents." Around 1885 they began to assemble one Tuesday every month at the Restaurant Riche for "Impressionist" dinners.

The Restaurant Riche.

Ah! Oculus, the moment has come to try a new lock.

I swear by the name of Tom that I've never seen anything as marvellous as this series of Cathedrals of Rouen!

Monet rented an apartment on the square in Rouen, set up several easels in front of its windows, and painted four or five canvases at a time, going from one to another according to the hour. He stayed there for several months and brought back twenty paintings representing the same subject seen at different times of day. They're fascinating!

Notice how the cathedral changes in appearance, seeming real or imagined, imposed or insubstantial, all depending on how the light hit it at the moment it was painted. Monet observes, Monet makes real. The light falls differently on

Claude Monet, *Rouen Cathedral. Portal and Saint-Romain Tower, Morning Effect, Harmony in White*, 1894. Oil on canvas, 3 feet 6 inches × 2 feet 5 inches.

leaves and masonry, it reinvents materials and color. If the building becomes pinkish, bluish, yellow, or ochre, it is only an illusion created by the light. But Monet knows that that's what he sees in the moment he's painting the cathedral. So for him it is reality, the only truth of that particular moment.

What is new about this way of working?

Just about everything. Imagine a theater set with actors moving about in front of it. The director tells them where to move and asks the lighting designer to spotlight the central character. Traditional painters work in much the same way. They decide on the brightness and direction of the light. But Monet gives light itself the principal role, he kneels down before it: it is his star, his idol!

Claude Monet, *Rouen Cathedral. Portal in Morning Sunlight, Harmony in Blue*, 1894. Oil on canvas, 3 feet × 2 feet 1 inch.

What's the matter, Oculus? You seem a bit confused, a bit lost. Monet doesn't mean to make things difficult for you. It's just that he's faithful to what he sees and not what he knows. Some of his friends said of him that he was nothing but an eye! But he wasn't a beginner like you; he was a master.

So now we have to learn to look at forms in a new way. Before, every object and every figure had its own life: they were placed together on a single canvas and that was that. In *Alice Hoschedé in the Garden*, everything mixes and we have to set all the boundaries ourselves. The foliage blends with the sky, Alice's dress merges with the plants in the garden. You can't tell the climbing roses from the fence, and the small table seems almost to disappear. Everything bleeds together. Every square inch of canvas has its importance. What we see is a woman sewing under the shade of a tree in a garden on a specific summer day.

Do you see a little more clearly now, Oculus? Are you going to stop fluttering about like a crazed moth? Rest assured that you are not the first to feel dizzy in front of this canvas—mixing up the background and the foreground like this had never been done before.

One spring Monet started a canvas representing an oak, but poor weather forced him to stop working. When he returned to complete the painting, the oak was covered with leaves. Monet went to the mayor of the village and had the tree stripped of its foliage.

Claude Monet, *Alice Hoschedé in the Garden*, 1881. Oil on canvas, 2 feet 7 inches × 2 feet 2 inches.

Auguste Renoir, *The Swing*, **1876. Oil on canvas, 3 feet × 2 feet 5 inches.**

And here's a key to the temple garden, a key to the period if ever there was.

The door opens, without a sound, not the slightest creak. For here not a particle of dust, not even the faintest hint of rust, is to be found. Be careful, the paint's still wet!

Look at *The Swing*. It's a fine example of open-air painting. Oculus, could you imagine for even an instant that this painting was made in the studio? Renoir painted it exactly as the light showed him, depicting each figure as it appeared to him. It's lovely! It could be by me!

Renoir painted *The Swing* in the garden of his studio in the Rue Cortot. Mornings, he painted at the Moulin de la Galette, an open-air dance hall pictured here. Its name derived from the nearby windmills (*moulins*) and the little cakes (*galettes*) made on the premises.

Come on, let's swing in the swing.

Renoir loved to paint women; look at this one trying to keep her balance, looking away dreamily. Her white dress is a surface on which the sun creates a mosaic of white, pink, green, ochre, and blue. She is accompanied by two men, one of whom leans against a tree. Have you noted, Oculus, the kindness in the man's face, how full of happiness it is?

I always want to touch Renoir's canvases. Off limits! I'll get caught by a temple guard. But this artist's surfaces are so sensual they seem to invite a caress. Try, Oculus, to touch them with your eyes, and you'll see how they're soft like velvet. Look at the back of the man's jacket; here, light creates the shape. There's also a little girl painted touch by touch; she is both very much present and in the process of appearing, like a sketch. Other figures are visible further down the path covered with patches of light and shade. They're all blurry. However, a small touch of red that must be a flower in a lapel brings them to our attention. The longer one looks at this group, the better one can make out the poses and dress of its figures.

Let's have a little talk with them.

"Mesdames, Messieurs, Do you have the time? About three o'clock? That's just what I thought." You see, Oculus, this canvas represents a brief moment in the lives of these people. Now don't tell me you're getting sleepy! Open your eyes to the light! That's better.

Renoir is always in a good mood, he doesn't take life too seriously. He's not a man of theory. If we were to ask him what open-air painting was, he'd answer obligingly: "A marvellous invention in cahoots with a new idea."

Auguste Renoir, *The Swing*, detail.

The invention was paint tubes. Without it, no open-air painting! Before, painters mixed their own colors. Can you picture them with their pots of paints and their spatulas in the middle of the woods, trying to get just the right colors?

As for the new idea, that was to subject color to the fleeting influences of light, weather, and passing time.

I bet, Oculus, that when you want to preserve something you see you just pick up a camera and snap the shutter. Or, better yet, you shoot some footage with a movie camera. Everything's been made easy for you. The Impressionists, too, sought to capture brief moments and movement, but with an art that had previously been devoted to rendering people, landscapes, and objects immortal.

Oculus, let's transport ourselves into the studio of Frederic Bazille in 1867, for it affords a view of the studio of Eugene Delacroix, the master of Romanticism. Bazille and Monet, who were very good friends, watched their elder colleague at work and were astonished at what they saw. His models didn't pose, they walked and moved about. Delacroix made rapid sketches. It was only when he was alone again that he carefully worked up a figure.

Photography opened up new horizons for painters in the 19th century, especially after the discovery of a new chemical process that required less posing time, making it possible to photograph and preserve events that normally would be over in a instant. As a result, their—and our—vision of the world was altered. Félix Nadar, who knew many painters, was among the most audacious photographers of the period. He excelled at aerial and panoramic views and strove to document modern life. His subjects and framing strategies were similar to those of the Impressionists and appealed to them.

"One should be able to draw a man falling from the seventh floor," he once said. Just think how fast one would have to draw! All the same, I can think of less disturbing subjects to sketch.

Horse races, for example. They'd provide plenty of movement, as in this canvas. Delacroix would be happy with it, for he loved horses. These are by Edgar Degas. In this painting, there is both movement and expectation. The jockey in orange is galloping into the picture. Others seem about to head out of it. We see the back of a carriage, which is also pulling away.

Edgar Degas, *The Racecourse, Amateur Jockeys*, c. 1877–1880. Oil on canvas, 2 feet 2 inches × 2 feet 8 inches.

In 1878, when Degas was working at Longchamp, Eadweard Muybridge managed to capture on camera the actual steps made by a galloping horse, documenting its movements for the first time.

Dear Oculus, I invite you to spend an evening with Edgar Degas and his dancers. They're preparing to go on stage. You can't see anything but feet? That's just what you must look at. The young women warm up, try out a few steps, and, thanks to the point of view chosen by the painter, we are pulled down towards the floor, for that's where everything is happening. Degas depicts gestures from there, crying out: "No one has ever done monuments and houses from low down, from below, from close by, as they're seen in the streets." And it's true. Before him, compositions were framed and organized according to formulas developed during the Renaissance.

That might strike you as a bit complicated. Don't panic, I'll give you a little lesson in perspective. First of all, what is it? Perspective enables us to represent objects on a flat surface (paper, canvas) so that they seem three dimensional. When you look at the two parallel rails of a train track, you have the impression that they come together at the horizon. But you know that isn't the case, for that would wreck the train. It's an optical illusion that painters recreate to create an impression of depth in the works. In the language of perspective, the spot where the parallel lines seem to merge is called the vanishing point, and the horizontal line passing through it is called the horizon line.

Stop yawning, Oculus, painting isn't all a matter of little flowers!

In the Renaissance, artists pitched their easels at eye height, placed the horizon line half-way up the canvas, and organized their paintings around a central vanishing point.

Whatever they depicted was wholly within the painting; there was no question of slicing off a head, an arm, a leg or even an object at the frame.

Degas and other modern painters formulated new approaches to framing and perspective. They began to view their subjects from eccentric angles. They showed us the floor, fragmentary figures, and objects halfway off the canvas. Feet made a daring subject for paintings. In his pastel *The Green Dancers*, Degas is like us, a moving eye that turns and flies above the dancers, stopping suddenly to capture the blink of an eye or a fleeting movement. He was out to paint passing feelings and light, to get down a momentary impression.

Edgar Degas, *Dancers in Green*, 1877–1879. Pastel and gouache, 2 feet 2 inches × 1 foot 2 inches.

Let's explore the temple a bit, Oculus. Here are some arabesques. This cast-iron balcony is a bit like a curtain from behind which one can look at a performance without being seen. Bend down: a coach is passing by. Caillebotte has chosen an unexpected point of view for a painting but one that's quite commonplace in daily life, as when we await the arrival of a friend from behind a window or seated on a balcony.

Perhaps now you have a better sense of how the choice of a perspective or a point of view can create an impression of spontaneity. It's worth repeating, Oculus, that photography and Japanese art played important roles in the development of this new way of picturing space.

In 1862, a shop called "La Porte Chinoise" ("The Gateway to China") opened on the Rue de Rivoli in Paris. The Far East was becoming fashionable. Kimonos were all the rage, while Chinese and Japanese objects appeared in living rooms. Painters discovered the woodcuts of Katsushika Hokusai, Utamaro Kitagawa, and Ando Hiroshige, admiring their compositions, the dignity of their forms, and the purity of their colors. A Japanese pavilion at the Universal Exposition of 1867 further increased the interest in things from Japan.

Hokusai, *Two Fishing Boats on a Rough Sea*. Early 19th century.

Gustave Caillebotte, *The Balcony*, 1880. Oil on canvas, 2 feet 2 inches × 1 foot 9 inches.

"Down with goddesses and Greek columns! We want to paint our own century!" Are you going to the demonstration, Oculus? And why shouldn't we lend our voices to the protests of these long-haired, bearded, and mustachioed painters?

What subject matter does this 19th century hold out for us? Trains, railroad stations, cafés, theaters, and scenes of daily life. The broad Parisian boulevards rebuilt by Haussmann, along with their amusements, carriages, and pedestrians. It was the life of bustling crowds that attracted the Impressionists. Renoir went into the streets with his brother, who asked passers-by for directions. The artist, sketchbook and charcoal in hand, seized the moment to get them down on paper.

Auguste Renoir, *Place Clichy*, 1875. Oil on canvas, 1 foot 8 inches × 2 feet.

A platform, a train. It's the Saint-Lazare railway station. Should we wave goodbye? Is someone leaving? No, they're arriving. And Monet was there. He had put on his best jacket, taken up his gold-tipped cane, and paid a courteous visit to the man in charge of the railway. Why? To ask his permission to paint in the station. His request was granted, and the result was a series of canvases in which the painter managed to capture the subtle effects created by the mixture of smoke and light.

Claude Monet, *The Gare Saint-Lazare*, 1877. Oil on canvas, 2 feet 6 inches × 3 feet 5 inches.

Wearing our own straw hats, we pass though the last gate. We're in a superb garden. It's immense, magnificent, there are forests, lakes, fields, everything one could wish for. It's the garden of the world. For don't forget, Oculus, the Impressionists were above all landscape painters and promoters of a free art. They took their inspiration from the rhythms of the seasons. In spring, summer, winter, and fall they were out in the open. Neither rain nor wind nor snow was enough to prevent them.

Note well, Oculus, that an artist's life is not a calm one. Umbrellas and heavy coats are essential tools for them. The Impressionists were at the mercy of light, and when night began to fall too early in the winter, Monet would furiously throw his paints into the mud or the sea.

As for Sisley, he loved the snow. He used delicate tints. His touch is subtle and delicate.

Renoir prefered the colors of the rainbow. All the Toms in the world couldn't equal the brilliance of his palette. How the fairies mocked me when they handed out their gifts, Oculus! How pale I seem beside Renoir!

Color as Ingres used it is now nothing but a memory. As the years passed, color was to become ever more important for ambitious artists. Gauguin, Van Gogh, and the painters known as the *fauves* or wild beasts would unleash its powers to an even greater extent.

Alfred Sisley, *Louveciennes in the Snow*, 1874. Oil on canvas, 1 foot 10 inches × 1 foot 6 inches.

There we are, Oculus, our expedition is nearing its end. We must leave the temple. Today we both have admired paintings that are priceless. And yet these poor Impressionists had to endure hostile criticism. At times they barely had enough to eat. Several of them—Monet, Sisley, Pissarro—suffered periods of great misery. What little they possessed they used to buy canvases and paints. And to think that their paintings provoked laughter . . .

I've turned over my keys. Unfortunately, I can't tap them on the shoulder and say, "Don't worry, everything will work out, one day your paintings will be worth millions!" But we have learned that artists are often in advance of their own time. It's up to us, Oculus, to do our best to see as far ahead as they do.

Happy looking.

Lives
of the
Impressionists

Camille Pissarro
(1830–1903)

Pissarro and Cézanne.

Pissarro was in a sense the spiritual anchor of the Impressionists. He was gentle, yet he managed to hold the painters together: it was thanks to his determination that there were eight Impressionist exhibitions. He is the only artist who took part in all of them.

He was born in the Antilles and showed a taste for drawing from a very young age. He was twenty-five when he arrived in Paris. It was the year of the Universal Exposition, where he discovered Delacroix, Corot, Courbet, Daubigny, and Millet. He attended the studio school known as the Académie Suisse, where he met Cézanne, Monet, and Guillaumin.

He started to paint in the open air, setting up his easel in Montmartre, on the banks of the Seine, and in the suburbs around Paris. He went with Monet, Renoir, Sisley, and Bazille to Fontainebleau Forest, the preferred site of the Barbizon painters. He sought the advice of Corot, whom he admired.

The war of 1870 dispersed the painters. Pissarro went to England, where he was soon joined by Monet. Together they studied the English landscapists Turner and Constable.

On returning to France, he settled in Pontoise and worked with Cézanne, initiating him into the mysteries of open-air painting. Pissarro painted nature as he saw it but in 1885, under the influence of Seurat, he began to use the pointillist technique of laying dots of pure color side by side to form a painting. After working in this meticulous and systematic style for four years, he reverted to his old way of painting.

Édouard Manet
(1832–1883)

Manet was the founding figure who started the revolution in painting.

Yet Manet was born into a middle class family, and in adult life he was a dandy obsessed by the figure he cut in society. His goal was to obtain the Legion of Honor, but while this ambition was strong he did not want to compromise his art to attain it.

He studied in the studio of Thomas Couture from 1850 to 1856.

He admired Francisco Goya, Diego Velázquez, Frans Hals, and Delacroix. He imitated their luminous black colors and the freedom of their brushstrokes. He also copied works by the old masters in the Louvre. It was there that he met Degas, who became his good friend. They both loved Ingres and admired his superb draftsmanship.

Manet as photographed by Nadar.

Manet's approach to composition was inspired by classical artists like Raphael.

In 1859, he submitted his *Absinthe Drinker* for exhibition at the Salon. It was not accepted.

But in 1861 his *Spanish Guitarist* met with great success. This work was noticed by the critics as well as by young artists and writers. Before long he had made friends with Baudelaire, Zola, and Stéphane Mallarmé.

In 1863, he showed his *Luncheon on the Grass* at the Salon des Refusés, or exhibition of rejected artists; the canvas provoked a scandal, but it stamped him as the head of the new school of painting.

Another scandal erupted in 1865, when his *Olympia* was exhibited at the Salon.

From 1873 to 1874, Manet worked with Renoir and Monet. His palette became lighter, and he developed a taste for the open air. His art blossomed, taking on a new life.

He was already admired by painters and intellectuals, but

Honore Daumier, *In Front of the Painting by Manet*, lithograph.

the coveted Legion of Honor was bestowed on him only later, in 1881, after he had fallen ill, and his pleasure in this recognition was clouded by bitterness. He died in 1883.

Edgar Degas
(1834–1917)

Doubtless Degas would lift his eyebrows if he saw us talking about him as an "Impressionist." He categorically refused this tag, and in fact he painted very few open-air landscapes, preferring to work in the artifical light of his studio. Drawing was his god, and he had great admiration for Ingres.

He was born into a wealthy family, and his father took him to see works of art owned by his collector friends. At the house of one of them, Valpincon, Degas met Ingres. Upon learning that he intended to devote his life to painting, Ingres said to him, "Make lines, young man, lots of lines, both from memory and after nature, that's the way to become a good painter."

Degas followed this advice, going often to the Louvre to draw after the old masters. There he met Manet, with whom he became friends. In this period Degas was interested in historical subject mat-

Degas

ter. But beginning in 1860 he abandoned such themes, turning instead to scenes from everyday life. He was also interested in the world of the theater, with its dancers and musicians, and that of the track, with its horses. He was a regular at the Café Guerbois, where he met Monet, Renoir, Sisley, Pissarro, and Cézanne. In 1874, he exhibited with them under the name Independent Artists. Degas showed his work at seven of the eight exhibitions.

Towards the end of his life he abandoned oils for pastels and began to make sculpture.

Paul Cézanne
(1839–1906)

Cézanne was always a bit rough at the edges. While he showed at two of the Impressionist exhibitions, like Degas he was somewhat distant from the group. He didn't mind being called an Impressionist, and he even said, "I'd like to make Impressionism into a living art." But his technique, approach, and subject matter all set him apart from the movement.

His handling was coarse, his surfaces were rough, and he liked broad fields of color. He was born in Aix-en-Provence, where Zola was a schoolmate. They both went to Paris, dreaming of becoming a painter and a writer, respectively. But Cézanne met with disappointment: he was not accepted into the Ecole des Beaux-Arts. So he studied at the Académie Suisse, where he met Pissarro.

He remained in Paris for a year, after which he returned to Aix to work in his father's bank.

But his devotion to painting led him once more to Paris. There he rejoined Pissarro, who introduced him into the rebellious circle based in the studio of Charles Gleyre. More than any stylistic agenda, these artists shared a desire to recast art in a more contemporary form. In 1873–1874 Cézanne worked with Pissarro, who encouraged him to lighten his palette and focus on landscape painting.

Thanks to the fortune left him by his father in 1886, Cézanne was able to pursue his art without financial worry, but he only became famous towards the end of his life.

Cézanne is an artist of forceful personality, and his art does not follow any one style despite the care with which it was constructed. Later artists, most notably the fauves and the cubists, would see him as a stylistic precursor.

Cézanne, The House of the Hanged Man, 1873. Oil on canvas, 1 foot 10 inches × 2 feet 2 inches.

Alfred Sisley
(1839–1899)

Sisley was without doubt the quietest member of the group, and his art is delicate and subtle. His early years as a painter were unusually easy, for his father, a rich English businessman based in France, was not opposed to his chosen vocation. During a voyage in England from 1857 to 1862, he discovered Constable and Turner. He then, studied with Gleyre, the Swiss painter whose studio was then a base of operations for Renoir, Bazille, and Monet. Encouraged by the latter, he began to paint in the Fontainebleau Forest.

His father died bankrupt, and as a result Sisley had to face difficult financial problems. Although he was taken up by the Impressionist group very early on, he was never as successful as his friends, and this depressed him. But he never lost his enthusiasm for painting. He worked mostly in the Seine valley and adjacent sites: Marly, Bougival, Sèvres, and Suresnes.

Sisley around 1872.

Claude Monet
(1840–1926)

W ho was this man who so loved light and its various effects that he devoted everything to it: his time, his life, and his eyes?

Monet was born in Paris but spent his youth in Le Havre. He began his career drawing caricatures. Initially this occupation was only a hobby, but he received so many requests that he decided to charge 20 francs per portrait. When he was seventeen, his work was shown in the window of a framer along with seascapes by Eugène Boudin. This encounter was important, for it was under Boudin's guidance that Monet executed his first open-air canvases. Four years later, Boudin introduced him to Jongkind.

At age nineteen, Claude set out for Paris to study painting. He registered at the Académie Suisse, where he met Pissarro. Then, at the urging of his family, he began to study with Charles Gleyre, where he allied himself with Bazille, Re-

Monet as photographed at the end of his life by Sacha Guitry.

noir, and Sisley, all of whom resisted Gleyre's teachings.

It was he who brought his friends to the Fontainebleau Forest, where they met the Barbizon painters. Between 1862 and 1864 he painted in the outdoors, first at Le Havre and then at Honfleur with Boudin and Jongkind. In 1873 he settled in Argenteuil, where he set up a floating studio and painted with Renoir and Monet. In 1874 it was his canvas *Impression, Sunrise* that gave the name "Impressionists" to the group of independent exhibiting artists.

Much of Monet's life was difficult. He was often reduced to asking friends to buy his work so that he could eat. His work was long misunderstood by the public and the critics, but he never compromised. In his artistic quest, he made ever greater efforts to capture first impressions, what the eye perceives when it first takes in the landscape. His series paintings are proof of this.

In 1879 his companion Camille, with whom he had had two sons, died. He threw himself into his work. In 1883 he moved to Giverny with Madame Hoschedé, who became his second wife.

Little by little, the financial difficulties disappeared, and Monet became much admired during the last decades of his life.

In Giverny he created a garden as remarkable as his paintings. He depicted it in many canvases, especiallly the waterlillies in its pool. In these mesmerizing paintings his genius was given free reign, erupting in an explosion of color.

Monet died blind in 1926.

Waterlilies. Clouds, **detail from central panel.**

Berthe Morisot
(1841–1895)

Berthe Morisot had a pale face in which shone two big black eyes framed by thick dark hair. Although her physical presence was marked by stark contrasts, her art was reticent and discreet.

Morisot's father, Prefect of the Cher and an extremely cultivated man, gave his daughters drawing lessons. Berthe's gifts were soon apparent, and her parents sent her to study with the painter Guichard. While copying works in the Louvre, she met Fantin-Latour and was offered advice by Corot. In 1868 she attracted the attention of Manet, who asked her to pose for him.

In 1874 she married Manet's brother Eugène. That same year she took part in the first exhibition of the Impressionist group. She showed at all of its exhibitions except the fourth, when pregnancy prevented her. Unlike the other Impressionists, Morisot did not create patches of contrasting col-

B. Morisot, *The Cradle*, 1873. Oil on canvas, 1 foot 10 inches × 1 foot 6 inches.

ors but instead distributed her colors over the canvas with delicacy and confidence and without challenging the integ-

rity of individual forms. At the end of her life, like Renoir, she laid even greater stress on conventional drawing.

Pierre Auguste Renoir

(1841–1919)

This angular face hides a simple man full of joy and optimism. His life was shaped by his love for painting, women, and his children.

Renoir was thirteen when he began to work in a small porcelain factory in Limoges. There he learned to decorate plates and cups with floral motifs. But the factory closed, and Pierre Auguste had to find a job. Thanks to his natural gifts for painting, he soon found work as a decorator. He managed to put aside enough money to attend the Ecole des Beaux-Arts and study with Charles Gleyre. When his schedule allowed, he went to the Louvre and copied paintings by Rubens, Boucher, Watteau, and Fragonard.

In Gleyre's studio he met Monet, Sisley, and Bazille. This group began to frequent the Café Guerbois, a gathering place for young artists. Renoir wasn't much of a talker, he preerred to listen to his friends. It was here that the idea of a Society of Independent Artists was born. Renoir took part in the first such exhibition, which was held in 1874 in the former studio of the photographer Félix Nadar. There would be seven more such shows. In all, Renoir displayed works in four of these exhibitions.

He painted with Monet at Bougival, on the banks of the

Renoir as photographed by Lefevre.

Seine, and at La Grenouillère. He also worked in the open air with Sisley and Bazille. At one point, financial difficulties obliged him to share a studio with Bazille.

In 1872 he met Paul Durand-Ruel, a picture dealer. He was supportive of the Impressionists and helped make them more popular. But their beginnings were difficult, and they sold few paintings.

Renoir managed to survive thanks to a few portrait commissions, but he preferred to paint women. He said: "I loved women even before I had learned to walk." At age forty he married Aline Charigot, who had been his companion for ten years. He had three children with her: Pierre, who became an actor; Jean, who became a movie director; and Claude, who as a child was his favorite model.

In 1907–1909 he built a house at Cagnes-sur-Mer. At the end of his life, his hands were completely deformed by rheumatism and he was often in great pain. But he never stopped painting.

GLOSSARY

arabesque: a complicated pattern of intertwined lines

Barbizon painters: a group of painters living in the village of Barbizon, located in northern France, who painted landscapes outdoors rather than in a studio

caricaturist: a person who draws humorous portraits by exaggerating the features of his or her subjects

classicism: a school of painting emphasizing balance, realism, and imitation of Greek or Roman styles and subject matter

Impressionism: a school of painting that used dabs or strokes of unmixed color to simulate actual reflected light

Independant Artists: a loose association of artists who in 1874 gave the first exhibition of what are now called Impressionist paintings

palette: the array of colors used by a particular painter

pointillism: a style of painting in which small strokes or dots of color are placed next to each other on a canvas so that from a distance they seem to blend together

Renaissance: a period in Europe, ranging from the 14th to the 17th century, in which the arts were dominated by classicism

romanticism: a school of painting that emphasized emotion, bold colors, and non-classical subject matter but was still very realisitic

Salon: an annual exhibition of art in Paris; to be exhibited an artist had to be chosen by a notoriously conservative jury

Salon des Refusés: an exhibition, established by Napeleon III in 1863, of artists who had been excluded from the Salon

Where Are the Works in This Book?

p. 8: Jean-Dominique Ingres, *La Grand Odalisque*, 1814. Paris, Musée du Louvre, c RMN.

p. 9: Eugène Delacroix, *Lion Hunt*, 1855. c Kunsthalle, Bremen.

p. 11: Édouard Manet, *Le Déjeuner sur l'herbe*, 1863. Paris, Musée d'Orsay. c RMN.

p. 13: Johan-Barthold Jongkind, *Entry to the Port at Honfleur*, 1863. Paris, Musée d'Orsay. c RMN.

p. 15: John Constable, *Clouds*, 1822. c National Gallery of Victoria, Melbourne, Felton Bequest.

p. 16: J.M.W. Turner, *Rain, Steam and Speed—The Great Western Railway*, 1844. c The National Gallery, London.

p. 19: Claude Monet, *Impression, Sunrise*, 1872. Paris, Musée Marmottan. c RMN.

p. 20: Auguste Renoir, *The Boating Party*, 1881. c The Phillips Collection, Washington, D.C.

p. 23: Édouard Manet, *Argenteuil*, 1874. Musée des Beaux-Arts de Tournai, c Photorob, Tournai (p. 22, detail).

p. 25: Claude Monet, *The Bridge at Argenteuil*, 1874. Paris, Musée d'Orsay. c RMN (p. 24, detail).

p. 26: Camille Pissarro, *Boulevard Montmartre, Night Effect*, 1897. c The National Gallery, London.

p. 28: Claude Monet, *Rouen Cathedral. Portal and Saint-Romain Tower, Morning Effect, White Harmony*, 1894. Paris, Musée d'Orsay. c RMN.

p. 29: Claude Monet, *Rouen Cathedral. Portal in Morning Light, Blue Harmony*, 1894. Paris, Musée d'Orsay. c RMN.

p. 31: Claude Monet, *Alice Hoschedé in the Garden*, 1881. Private collection.

p. 32: Auguste Renoir, *The Swing*, 1876. Paris, Musée d'Orsay. c RMN.

p. 35: Auguste Renoir, *The Swing*, detail. Paris, Musée d'Orsay. c RMN.

p. 36: Daumier, *Nadar Elevating Photography to the Heights of Art*. c Bibliothèque Nationale, Paris.

p. 37: Edgar Degas, *The Racecourse, Amateur Jockeys*, 1877–1880. Paris, Musée d'Orsay. c RMN.

p. 39: Edgar Degas, *Dancers in Green*, 1877–1879. Thyssen-Bornemisza Collection, Lugano.

p. 40: Katsushika Hokusai, *Two Small Fishing Boats in a Rough Sea off the Choshi Coast, in the Province of Shimosa*, early 19th century. Huguette Berès Collection, Paris.

p. 41: Gustave Caillebotte, *The Balcony*, 1880. Private collection.

p. 42: Auguste Renoir, *The Place Clichy*, 1875. c Fitzwilliam Museum, Cambridge.

p. 43: Claude Monet, *The Gare Saint-Lazare*, 1877. Paris, Musée d'Orsay. c RMN.

p. 45: Alfred Sisley, *Louveciennes in the Snow*, 1874. c The Phillips Collection, Washington, D.C.

p. 50: Honoré Daumier, *In Front of the Painting by Manet*, c Bibliothèque Nationale, Paris.

p. 52: Paul Cézanne, *The House of the Hanged Man in Auvers*, 1873. Paris, Musée d'Orsay. c RMN.

p. 55: Claude Monet, *Waterlillies, Clouds*. Paris, Musée de l'Orangerie. c Lauros-Giraudon.

p. 56: Berthe Morisot, *The Cradle*, 1873. Paris, Musée d'Orsay. c RMN.

Photographic Credits

p. 21: The Restaurant Fournaise, c Sipa Press. Photo Perreire.
p. 27: The Café Riche, c Roger-Viollet—Collection Viollet.
p. 30: Monet in his garden, c Photographic Service, Sénépart.
p. 33: The windmills of Montmartre, c Sipa icono. Photo Goldner.
p. 48: Pissarro and Cézanne, c Roger-Viollet.
p. 49: Manet as photogaphed by Nadar, c Caisse des Monuments Historiques, Paris.
p. 51: Degas, c Harlingue-Viollet.
p. 54: Monet as photographed at the end of his life by Sacha Guitry, c Harlingue-Viollet.